Experiencing the Light

Stories of Resilience and Redemption You'll Never Forget

By Susan Pyron

In association with Bill Laney

Table of Contents

This book is dedicated to

Sukie and Jim with love and gratitude for their patience and support and to Ann Adams for her loving guidance and wisdom
and
In loving memory of Carla Dowler

Introduction

Bill and I love stories. Everybody has one, but since no two people live the same life, every person's story is uniquely theirs. None of us can have every life experience, but we can gain insights, knowledge, and inspiration from reading the stories of people who have had experiences both similar and vastly different from our own.

This is a collection of true stories told by people who have faced a variety of life's challenges. While the circumstances of each story varies, the one constant is that the person in the story was either sustained or transformed by their faith in Jesus.

John 8:12 says *When Jesus spoke again to the people, he said, "I am the light of the world. Whoever follows me will never walk in darkness but will have the light of life."*

Every person in this book either fell into darkness or had such trauma or loss that they might have turned away from God. A couple of them hit bottom before they realized the only way out of the darkness was to walk toward the light and accept Jesus into their lives.

As you read these people's stories, notice that many had lost their way. Look for the themes of trust, resilience, and redemption. As a four-time survivor of cancer, I know it takes a lot of faith to be resilient and trust that everything is going to be all right. From sitting with some of the subjects in this book, I learned that it takes a lot of humility to ask God to show the way out or to ask, "God, will you take me back?"

While you're reading, notice the role of fathers and father figures. Take note of the "I've been there" moments or the "thank goodness that wasn't me" moments. Watch for the moments when God sends the right person at the right time.

Hopefully, one or more of these stories will touch something in you and start you thinking about your own story and where you are in your faith journey. If you are in the midst of a trying time in your life, I hope you are inspired by the subjects in this book who have overcome abuse, addiction, ancestral trauma, medical issues, and unimaginable tragedy. So can you if you walk toward the light.

Susan

A Word of Caution

Some of these stories are hard to read and could trigger an emotional reaction from you if you have experienced violence, trauma, or the loss of a child. As you are reading, be assured that all the subjects in this book are not merely doing well but thriving and contributing to their communities. I have written an introduction to most of the stories that hint at what is in that story so you can decide if you want to continue reading. Please be kind to yourself as you read.

Lori
Which Way to Go

Years ago, our young family went to Telemark Resort in northern Wisconsin for a weekend of play. One warm Saturday afternoon, I left our two sons in the care of my husband for some "mom-time" mountain biking. I was excited to have the afternoon to myself. Knowing the vast expanse of hilly trails from winter cross-country skiing, I confidently set out with my bike and water bottle ready to enjoy the afternoon.

After an hour or so of riding, I saw a sign that said, "Leaving Telemark Property." I felt a bit disconcerted, as I thought I knew where I was, and I had never seen a Telemark boundary sign before. I stopped and drank my water, feeling a bit weak from the ride and the confusion.

Wishing I had brought a map, I decided to try retracing my steps. The trails were overgrown with thick foliage. Though I had skied this area many times and knew the snowy terrain very well, the forest looked so different in the summertime! I realized I was totally lost. I had no food, no water, and no cell phone. I began to worry. I should have brought another bottle of water, a protein bar, and a cell phone. And a map! Why didn't I plan more carefully?

I rode my bike on and on with no sight of any familiar landmarks. Eventually, I came across another "Leaving Telemark Property" sign. With every twist and turn, and with

5

every choice of trail, I became more and more frightened. I was thirsty, and exhausted, and my body was shaky.

At the next crossroad I just stopped. I knew I was in trouble, hopelessly lost amidst all these trees. I couldn't continue biking without any direction. I cried out to the Holy Spirit, "Please show me which way to go. I don't know where I am. I'm lost. Please help me!" At that moment, I heard an aircraft. I remembered there was a small airstrip near the Telemark Lodge. Looking up, I saw an airplane turn, dipping its wing downward to the right. My gaze followed its wing that pointed to a sign partially hidden by foliage. It read, "To Telemark," and I instantly knew in which direction to go! "Thank you," I whispered.

I only had about two more miles to go. My worried husband greeted me at the door. I had been gone for four hours! I knew I wanted nothing more than to be right there with him and my family. I was home at last!

Reflection:

- **Think about a situation where you felt lost in your life and didn't know what to do next. Where did you turn for help?**

- **Lori said a prayer and instantly heard an airplane, which gave her a clue how to get out of the woods. What has been your experience with prayer? Do prayers always get answered right away? When have you gotten an answer that was different from what you wanted?**

Susan
Experiencing a Father's Love

When I was in college and living in a dorm, I usually made a trip home to my small town in northern North Carolina when my dirty clothes outnumbered my clean ones. On one such fall weekend; I arrived home after dark. There was a light misty rain, so I pulled close behind my mother's car in our carport to unload my car without getting wet. My dad came out with a big smile to greet me just as I was stepping out of the car.

Suddenly his expression turned intensely serious, and he said, "Susan, stop! Look at me and don't take your eyes off my face. I need you to do exactly what I tell you to do." If it had been anyone else, I would have immediately demanded an explanation. But it wasn't anyone else. It was my dad. My dad who didn't tease or play jokes, who rarely issued commands or spoke sternly. He was very calm, but the look on his face told me I needed to follow every direction precisely. We proceeded to do something resembling a game of Simon Says with him directing me to take giant steps and baby steps until I was standing right in front of him.

When I asked why we did that, he put his hands on my shoulders and turned me around. My knees became weak at what I saw. I had parked beside a tangle of baby snakes – highly venomous copperhead snakes! Because our house was surrounded by wooded lots, we had seen an occasional snake, but never like this. In addition to the tangle of snakes, there were about 8-10 little snakes in my path to the back door. If I had stepped out onto the driveway carrying a load of laundry on that dark, rainy night, I likely would have been bitten. My dad's calm, steady voice guided me around the snakes to safety. I trusted him and, at that moment, knew I needed to obey.

In my story, I was in danger and didn't know it. One wrong step and I would have been in serious trouble. I trusted my father so much that I didn't look down to see what was causing his concern, and I didn't question his directions. I knew that he was guiding my steps for some reason he could see, and I couldn't.

Reflection:

- **What is the relationship between the words *faith* and *trust*? Are they the same thing or are there shades of difference?**

- **How does this story relate to our relationship with God as our heavenly father?**

- **What makes it hard to put all your trust in God?**

Jack
Finding My Purpose

Although I never met Jack, I had three telephone interviews with him arranged by a friend who also lives in West Palm Beach. When we talked, Jack was good-natured and had a smile in his voice that belied any previous problems, but he had had nothing but problems the first half of his life.

Jack came from an old Mississippi family with a famous name and a history of wealth and power. He grew up in the Catholic Church and had parents with high expectations. Although Jack tried, he could never measure up. Every time his attempts to please his parents failed, he turned to alcohol. By the time he was in his twenties, alcohol had become his lord and master, and his faith was a thing of the past.

The events of the ensuing years were exhausting and self-defeating as he tried to put his life together and repeatedly got knocked down through self-sabotage or by circumstances out of his control. Thirty years after he graduated from high school, his parents had died, his friends had grown weary of his destructive behavior, and he had absolutely no prospects of a productive future. He did have a little money left from his inheritance that he had not blown. Then God, who had not forgotten Jack, even though Jack had forgotten Him, stepped in…

From the Brink of Death to a New Life

In 1999, I realized my money wasn't going to last forever. I was getting older and had nothing and nobody to live for, so I decided to commit suicide. But what was the best way to kill myself? I went out to my front porch and sat down to decide how to end my life. While sitting there, I saw a young man clumsily riding a bicycle down my road. "What an idiot!" I thought. He wobbled and swerved awkwardly until he got right in front of my house, abruptly stopped, and fell over. I yelled to him, "What happened?" He replied that his chain had come off. I knew I could fix that, so I grabbed some tools, went out to the street, and put his chain back in place. When he left, I decided it was too late to kill myself that day. I would wait until tomorrow.

The next day, I went back to the porch to resume my plans for committing suicide. Before long, two young men showed up with broken bicycles asking if I could fix them. It turned out I could. The next day, there were two more, the next day even more, and they kept coming. It seemed a lot of people needed their bikes fixed, and that I was getting a reputation for being able to help them.

I had just a little money left. Maybe, just maybe, I could open a bike shop. Maybe there was a future for me after all. All my life, there had been so many "maybes." I had followed so many possibilities and none of them had worked out. I had spent my life trying to fit into my parents' view of what I should be, but this was different. It felt right.

All the people coming to me for bike repairs were from a poor working neighborhood. There were many Guatemalan immigrants who depended on bicycles for transportation. Sensing this was where I was supposed to be, I rented a building in their neighborhood, took my tools, and went to work. Over the years, my business began to grow, and in 2007, I started a nonprofit called "Jack the Bike Man" where we not only fix bikes but also repair donated bikes and give them away to deserving people. We also started a program in which people can work in our shop for a designated number of hours to earn a new bike.

Twenty years after opening our first bike shop, we now have a warehouse with over a dozen repair stations and thousands of bicycle parts, and we recently broke ground for a new building. Over the years, we have given away over 34,000 bicycles and helmets to underprivileged children, the homeless, women re-entering society from prison, recovering addicts in halfway houses, and people living below the poverty line. Our programs have expanded to include teaching bike safety, repair, and maintenance. The bike shop is open seven days a week, and there is never a day we don't receive at least one donated bike. The bikes come from everywhere, and we find a deserving person for each one.

Was it a coincidence a young man struggling with his bike just happened to collapse right in front of my house on the very day I considered suicide as a solution to my life's problems? I don't think so. He could have fallen over anywhere along my street, but he didn't, he fell right in front of my house. I had been picked up and supported so many times. It was my turn to lift people up. Even though I felt I had no one, I was never alone. God was with me when I was down and out, and He is with me now. I found the purpose God had for me, and I feel richly blessed every day.

Reflection:

- Some people think everything is a coincidence; others think nothing is a coincidence, while others think it's a mixture. What is your opinion on coincidences?

- Give an example of something in your life that might have been a coincidence, but you think was a God-sent sign.

- Jack finally found out where he was supposed to be and what he was supposed to do. How can you discover your purpose? How do you know when you're where you are where you are supposed to be?

Jason

Climbing out of the Family Pit

The first time I saw Jason, he and another man were giving a demonstration of extreme fitness to a group of inner-city youth. After the program, the teenage boys swarmed around him like he was a rock star. When I commented to the man beside me that Jason certainly had a way with kids, he told me who Jason's grandfather was. Wow. What a heavy burden to carry. I studied him closely. Jason was smiling while calmly talking and joking with the boys. Although he gave no sign of it, he must have had a tough life with such an infamous grandfather. I wanted to know his story, and it turned out he was willing to tell it.

The Family Secret

I grew up in a small Ohio town living with my mother and a man I called Dad, but my last name was different from theirs. I didn't know much about my biological father because we never met. He sent me letters and, occasionally, he would call me. Through those calls, I gradually learned more about him.

My dad lived a tough life because of what his father had done. Throughout his life, he had a hard time maintaining relationships and holding down a job. People would beat him up because of his name. He would go into a bar to have a drink, the door would lock behind him, and the fighting would start. Finally, at age 37, he committed suicide. Even though I never met him, his death was a blow to me. If someone was never there, how could you miss them? Yet I did. I even took some of the blame as a child. I thought if he had just come back to Ohio like he said he might, or if he had called me, things would have been different. So many ifs. So much sadness.

My mother would not talk to me about my grandfather and wouldn't allow his name to be spoken in the house. She said his name was a cuss word. I would hear his name shouted when my mom and stepdad argued, or overhear whispers about the "mind controller," but no one would talk to me about him. It was a secret we had to keep. Nobody was supposed to know we were related to him.

One day in eighth grade, my whole life changed. I walked into history class and stared at the single name written on the chalkboard. Why was my grandfather's name on the board? What did my grandfather do to warrant a place in history class? I found out what the big secret was that day, and by the end of the day, everyone in school knew it too. The name on the chalkboard?

Charles Manson, the most notorious cult leader and self-proclaimed mind controller in American history. Everything fell into place. The big family secret. My family had tried to shield me from the facts of my ancestry, but more people knew than I had imagined.

After I was exposed as Charles Manson's grandson, I was bombarded with questions I couldn't answer. As some friends dropped away, feelings of frustration and rejection grew. At that middle school age when every child was changing and trying to figure out who they were, my feet were suddenly knocked out from under me. My world was shaken. It was all too much to process.

In Trouble

The issue of dealing with my grandfather's notoriety collided with problems I was already having in school. As a child, I had a significant stutter in addition to being dyslexic and hyperactive. The kids at school bullied me a lot. I got knocked down and would get back up, only to get knocked down again. This left me timid and shy about speaking and somewhat nervous and afraid of other people.

When I was eleven, my stepdad started teaching me boxing and mixed martial arts. He and I would go down to the basement every night and practice. It turned out I was good at it, very good. As we worked out and practiced, I got stronger and quicker. He also taught me the martial arts rules of conduct that we don't start fights, but we use our skills to defend ourselves or others. By the end of middle school, my childhood bullies had no idea what I could do to them if they bullied me or my friends.

It was about that age I began to get in trouble outside of school and landed in the juvenile court system. What had started as childhood mischief with my neighborhood friends had elevated to more serious escapades that involved the police. I was getting into fights that caused some serious injuries. When I started fighting, it seemed like a fog came over me, and I would hit and hit and hit until my opponent was badly hurt. Because of my poor impulse control and ferocious fighting, I spent 28 days of my eighth-grade year in juvenile detention.

In the ninth grade, a known bully challenged me to an after-school fight. I did not want to fight him, but he persisted. He had never lost a fight, so he had no idea what was going to happen. Once I started punching, I could not stop, and he ended up in the hospital. About a year later, I punched a guy so hard in the mouth that one of his teeth was embedded in my knuckles. I was no longer afraid of anybody; people were afraid of me.

Prison

After high school, I began selling drugs. I didn't think it was wrong because "everybody did it." When I was about 22 years old, I was charged with a felony. I had been receiving and sending marijuana in the mail, which is a federal crime. Now I was looking at prison. I was married and had a daughter. That marriage fell apart when my wife informed me I was not the father of the girl I thought was my daughter. That news only added to my frustration and anger.

Something had to change, and that change had to come from inside me. While I was in county jail awaiting transfer to prison, I noticed another prisoner doing something no one else was doing. He would always go back to his cell after chow time. I felt he knew something I didn't and asked if I could chat with him. The guy told me he was an ordained minister and shared that he was addicted to crack cocaine. He had relapsed after 20 years of being clean, and this evil drug landed him in jail. Then he started telling me about Jesus.

At that time, I had no relationship with God and didn't know anything about the Bible. The minister introduced me to Jesus that day and led me in a prayer inviting Jesus into my life. I had no clue what to expect when I asked Jesus to be a part of my life. I felt the presence of a higher power overwhelm me. As I lay in my cell that evening, I wept about my actions and my lifestyle and saw this trip to jail as being an eye-opener. God was moving into my life.

When it was time to be transported to prison, I was shackled to a tough-looking black man. On that bus ride, he told me I needed to "find my people" and join a gang as soon as possible if I was going to survive in prison. "My people. A gang." This did not sound good.

When we got to prison, they took us into a room, strip-searched us, then had us put on prison garb. After we were dressed, the big black man and I were again shackled together to go to our cells. As we walked down the hall, he commented on how muscular I was and quietly told me not to ever take off my shirt and show my muscles in this place because other prisoners would see me as a threat. He said they would come after me and try to take me down. The man told me again to find my people quickly. I couldn't be in his gang because they were all black, but he would help me in any subtle way he could. Prison was going to be worse than anything I had ever experienced.

When I first stepped into the prison yard, I saw many groups and recognized some guys from my neighborhood. They were all trouble. Trouble I did not want. I quickly realized if I joined a gang, any gang, I was going to become someone I didn't want to be. I turned around and headed to the chapel, but the chapel was empty. I wanted to know more about Jesus. Every day I ran laps at recreation time, then headed to the chapel to quietly pray and spend time with Jesus. I never joined a gang. I had no people. The big black man was true to his word and continued to advise me. Looking back, I see that even though I didn't really know God at that time, He had sent me some much-needed advice. I had Jesus and the wise counsel of that inmate, and that got me through my sentence. I vowed to never go back to prison.

Hitting Bottom and Climbing Out

In the years after prison, I was not living the life of a Christian, although I theoretically had accepted Jesus as my savior. I had detached myself from God.

I continued using and selling drugs but winning a boxing championship was my dream. I entered numerous boxing matches, and after many fights, I finally won the title. Then I failed the drug test, and my title was taken away. Even so, there was an article in the newspaper detailing my win.

Soon after that, I met Audrey, a nice Catholic girl with a strong faith. We moved in together and eventually got married. This was the point when I should have changed my life, but I kept on doing what I had always done. Audrey worked the second shift, and when she was at work, I continued to sell drugs and see other women. I drank too much and would get out of control at home. My wife and my children were starting to be afraid of me. Although divorce was not a word in Audrey's vocabulary, she was at a breaking point. This was not how she wanted to live and not how she wanted to raise her children.

Then one day something happened that shook me to the core. Many of my drug customers came to my house to pick up their drugs, but on this day, I made a delivery of cocaine to a man with a five-year-old son. As soon as the man got the cocaine, he began drawing lines on the table. His son ran up to him, saying, "Me, me, me, me, me." I looked at the man and said, "You're not going to give your boy cocaine, are you?" He replied that his son was born into this life, and he might as well start now. So yes, he was giving cocaine to his five-year-old. I had three young sons at this point and couldn't imagine giving them drugs. That child had no chance in life. He was caught in a vicious cycle, and I was contributing to that cycle. Was I doing the same to my own children?

I was back in a familiar spot. Something had to change, and I was the one who had to make that change. I was pushing God away. What did I need to do to get right with God?

For a long time, my priorities had been fighting, drugs, and women. I prayed to Jesus to show me the way out of the cycle of failing and getting back on my feet, only to fail again. My prayer was answered when I looked out the window and saw Audrey walking across the yard. If I was ever going to change my life, I needed to be with her. She was a beautiful, smart, kind, loving woman and an incredible wife and mother. I needed to change my ways to keep her. Looking back, I know God had sent her to me. She later told me that God kept putting Psalm 46:10 in her head, *"Be still, and know that I am God."* He was telling her to stay put. Just "be still" and let Him do His work.

That day Jesus led me out of the fight game, away from the drug trade, away from drinking, and back to the woman I needed in my life. I needed to let Jesus be my foundation and with His help and Audrey's support, I began to make a transition.

Finding Peace and Purpose

As I was driving down a road soon thereafter, I was overtaken by an urge to get rid of all the frustration, resentment, and anger I had bottled up inside me over the years. I pictured a large bag in my mind and one by one I mentally put all my grievances into that bag. I pulled over to the side of the road and got out of the car. I reached in, picked up my virtual bag, and flung it in a ditch. Then I got back into the car and left all that garbage behind. Finally, I was at peace with the Lord.

Up to that point, I had lived my life under the curse of my childhood stutter and the stigma of being Charles Manson's grandson. Finally, I was able to come out of the shadows and use my identity to help other boys who were born into disadvantaged circumstances. I started a nonprofit called Frontline Warrior Community Outreach. Our team works with at-risk young men and strives to make a difference in their lives using the principles of boxing and the love of a father figure to help them grow up to be respectful and responsible members of their community. We teach them they don't get to choose their family, but they can choose the people with whom they surround themselves. They don't have to sell drugs or fight and end up in prison like I did. They don't have to commit suicide like my dad. With God's help, our organization works to help them take control of their lives.

Now at age 45, I'm at peace with who I am. The more I turn my life over to God, the freer I become to accept His blessings. I have my loving wife Aubrey and four young sons who won't grow up feeling like they're not worthy. I use my experiences to help the young men in my ministry avoid the mistakes I made growing up. God changed my life, and I see His hand at work in these young men every day.

My life has come full circle. I had many, many painful challenges and disruptive struggles as a youth, but looking back, I would not change any of it, even the parts I am ashamed of. God was always with me, molding me, and pulling me toward a relationship with Him. I didn't see it. I didn't know it was happening, but He was always there, always faithful. By letting go of the past, I finally accepted the fact that God loves me unconditionally. He has truly given me peace and a purpose in my life.

Now many factors are working in my favor: my faith in God; my understanding of the Holy Spirit; my fellowship with other believers; the love of my family; and the opportunity to work with young men to break their cycle of poverty, drugs, and prison. I am at peace with what God has given me and feel free of the bonds of ancestral trauma.

Let God be your guide, follow your heart, and He will do the rest.

Reflection:

- Jason lived through some rough and dark times, often led by his frustration and anger. Through all this, where are the God moments? Where did people show up to guide Jason at the right time?

- There is a saying that the apple doesn't fall far from the tree, and throughout history, people have been categorized and judged by their family ancestry.

- How hard is it to rise above the reputation of an infamous ancestor or to live in the shadow of a famous ancestor?

Nancy
Homeless in Seattle

 If there ever was a person whose entire life story worked toward placing her right where she belonged, it is Nancy. She was raised by missionaries who traveled by boat to the islands off the coast of northwest Canada to minister to the indigenous people who lived on those islands. As an adult, she married, settled in British Columbia, and had three children.

When Bill met her, she was working as a receptionist for a Christian domestic violence counseling center in Seattle. Bill was on the Board of Directors of the organization, and during a meeting to discuss who the next director of the organization should be, one board member stated that the smartest person working there was the part-time receptionist. They called her into the meeting, and even though she was a full-time college student, they soon realized she was the perfect person for the job, and they gave it to her on the spot.

She went on to get both her master's degree in applied behavioral science and Doctor of Ministry. Over the following thirty years, she built the center into the largest Christian domestic violence facility in Washington and became a professor and an international speaker on domestic violence.

How she got to Seattle from her home in Canada is a dynamic example of how listening for the voice of God and stepping out in faith can transform a life.

There was a time when my life was marked with fear and confusion. I had a good job in accounting in a community I loved, a home on a beach on the west coast of Vancouver Island, family to help with the kids, and friends in whom to silently find refuge when things were dangerous and overwhelming. Then, I left my home country of Canada and crossed the border to get free from an abusive husband.

A Dream

The idea came to me in a dream one night. I was restless and, in my sleep, woke up wondering who I was wrestling with. I realized it was the Lord, and I sat up in bed and said, "What do you want?" Clear as anything, I heard *I want you to go to Seattle Pacific University*. I said, "Fine then. Now may I go back to sleep?"

When I woke up in the morning, I went to see my mom for coffee. She commented on how good I looked. It had been so long since anyone had said that as I'd been torn up inside. I hadn't told her I had secretly "left" my husband for an emotional rest and hadn't told her what I had experienced inside of our marriage. I was even preparing to go back to him a few days after I'd rested.

I told her about waking up and my experience with the Lord in the night. She said, "So, are you going to go?" I looked at her in shock. I thought to myself, "Leave Canada? Take my kids to the US where they don't know anyone? Leave my husband behind?" The absurdity of her comments shocked me, and I pushed back in confusion.

Then she said in a voice that was quiet and direct. "So, are you going to disobey the Lord?" I was undone.

Disobey the Lord? I knew it was His presence in the night. I knew it even as I talked with my mom. Mom and I knew our understanding of scripture included women's roles in marriage. Nothing made sense. I was so confused.

I returned home to my husband, but the violence escalated. My children were being threatened, and I knew I had to do something for all our sakes. I called the police and told them I had 'a friend' who was worried that her husband was making murderous threats, and she was scared. The police said they couldn't do anything unless something happened but said they could drive by her house to keep a watch out. Because of the nature of small-town gossip, I didn't want to give out my address, so I hung up, knowing help wasn't coming.

It was clearly up to me. I decided to follow the path the Lord had for me. I signed up for student housing at Seattle Pacific University and proceeded with a plan of moving. It was a leap of faith. Could I even get into school?

A Border Guard

I gave notice I was leaving my job and was moving. I packed what I could into my car along with my kids. We said goodbye to my family and drove off. I crossed the border late at night. With the kids asleep in their pajamas, I hoped I could slip into the United States undetected. I didn't have passports for the kids or permission from their dad to leave the country. I was still not prepared to close all doors in case things did not work out.

When I got to the border, I was waved aside by border patrol and asked to go inside. Once at the counter, they went through their usual questions: "Where are you going to stay in the US? How much money do you have? Why are you traveling at night? Where are you going to stay tonight? Do you have proof you have a meeting with SPU tomorrow? You must have a student visa to come into the United States and go to school. Do you have money in a bank account that you can prove you can afford to go to school and live in this country?"

I was taken aback by these endless questions and was unprepared. I kept replying hesitantly that I was only coming to investigate the possibility of coming to the US. Internally, I was deeply conflicted. What do I do if I can't get through? My parents would welcome me with open arms. But I was afraid my husband would find me and make good on his threats against us. I looked down at my beautiful children who'd been awakened in their sleep and looked confused. I wanted to be careful about what I said in front of them.

Finally, an exasperated border patrol guard pulled out a piece of paper. Looking at me with his piercing brown eyes, he passed me a pen, pointed to the paper, and commanded me to 'write down his name.' I frowned. "Whose name?" I replied. "You know exactly what I mean." He said, "Write down his name," he urged, "and I will personally make sure he never follows you. We will make sure he will always be denied access to this country."

Hesitantly, I looked at him and took the pen. I sighed a deep sigh as I looked first into the eyes of each of my children and then closed my eyes for a moment. The Lord was with me, in the wee hours standing at this bare, scratched counter with a glaring light across from a man whose demeanor changed from challenging to compassionate and protective. I wrote my husband's name: the man we were fleeing; the man I had loved; the father of our children; son of parents I adored; brother to in-laws I loved. It was bittersweet.

I knew we were going to be able to cross into the US, continuing to follow the Lord's direction. I was also full of grief. He'd not be able to follow me now, and things could get very bad! I was closing a door. We slept that night on the side of the road. We were tired, but we were safe, and it felt so good!

Homeless

We headed the next day to Seattle Pacific University, a beautifully treed campus. I had happy memories from a past visit, but it was all new to my kids. We needed to be settled, have a routine, and begin building a life in this place.

At the registrar's office, I was delighted to find I'd indeed been accepted into the School of Sociology and Anthropology. I registered for my classes, ignoring the looming tuition bill that would soon have to be paid. We splurged on lunch at the cafeteria and played on the grass. We walked along the banks of the canal that ran along the edge of the campus.

Our next stop was housing. Unfortunately, there was nothing available for us. I was in shock. Without housing, attending school would be impossible. Where would we live? I felt numb.

You cannot work as a Canadian in the US without a work or student visa. I tried applying for rentals and found lines of people all hoping their applications would be accepted. I could not provide references from a previous landlord, an American credit history, personal or work references, or a history of employment. Explaining my situation, everyone was very nice though one man offered his place in exchange for sexual favors as long as I kept it from his wife.

I was struggling. I was careful with my cash supply, but it was quickly dwindling. I'd heard from friends and family that my husband had realized I'd left him, taken the kids, and left no forwarding address. I was afraid for them as I knew what he was capable of. I could not go home.

Seattle is a beautiful city with lots of lakes and bodies of water. I would take the kids to these various places to play and to be outside. We enjoyed the goodness of strangers who shared cookies and crackers with my three friendly kids. My heart ached for them as we would drive through Burger King and order tall waters for everyone with lots of ice, with no money for happy meals and things they used to have. They never complained and found so much happiness playing with each other and other kids they met along the way. We found inside play areas for rainy days. We'd sleep in the car in lighted areas I'd scoped out. We'd sing and play I Spy. We'd listen to the radio and sleep like lambs. We were safe, and we had each other. It was almost fun. What was left for me was waiting for the Lord to show me the next step. I couldn't go back, but we couldn't sustain this living arrangement. School would start soon for all of us. It was odd – I felt both stuck and free. I waited.

The Kindness of Strangers

Reflecting on the life I left behind, I remembered a group of American men, women, and teenagers who had visited our community. They'd left their phone number recorded in a journal I kept. With the phone number was an invitation to come visit them if I was ever in Seattle. I found the number and decided to give them a call. I simply said, "Hi! We are in town for the weekend. Could we visit?" They warmly invited us to come see them and spend the weekend. They all lived in duplexes, single men on one side, and couples and single women on the other. It was wonderful to be in the company of friends, sleep in warm beds, and bathe.

As we prepared to leave on Monday morning, the four men asked to speak to me. They were professionals, athletic, single, and committed followers of Jesus. I was terrified as I sat down. We gathered in the small living room area, with the kids next door. It was unnerving. One man got down on one knee and asked outright if the kids and I would live with them. I was so shocked! I wondered to myself which one of the kids had spilled the beans. They had enjoyed the guys so much; they must've said something. My heart was pounding, and I could barely see. I managed to tell them in the most dignified way that I wasn't in an emotional place to live with one of them, let alone four of them. Shaking, I got up to leave. As I got up, another one of them got down on one knee. Taking off his hat, revealing a military haircut, he said earnestly, "The Bible says our religion is worthless if we don't take care of widows and orphans." With hot, blushing cheeks, surprised he would twist scripture like that, I replied, "I am not a widow, and my children are not orphans," to which he replied with emphasis, "That is a #### technicality." I understood.

I was so undone by their offer and their sincerity that I wish I could report that I said yes right away, but I was not able to. I was terrified and was too proud to receive their help and too confused by their kindness. I left. Learning of a shelter downtown where I could get some basic necessities and a place to sleep, I checked in there. The first night, I was directed to two single mattresses to push together to share with the kids. As we were settling in, older men came into the room to bed down for the night as well. One seemed to begin to inch his way in our direction. I picked up my daughter, grabbed the boys' hands, and left. I was devastated by the risk I took and shaken to think of how much safer I felt in my car than at a shelter.

Later, in a restaurant marked by a large elephant statue on the roof, we ordered water, hoping for crackers and crayons for kids to color their placemats. It was a hit. The waitress was fun and snuck a few extra packages of crackers into the basket on the table while we played. A young woman with two toddlers came over and asked if I was a single mom. "I'm not really sure," I said. She lowered her voice and said, "I just came up from Oregon. I saw my husband shoot and kill someone last night,

28

and I jumped in my car with the kids and took off. Here I am." Horrified, I asked her if she was okay, and she said she was, but she needed a favor. She wanted me to watch her kids in this restaurant for an hour so she could run an errand. It was urgent.

I looked at her closely. Her eyes were pleading, and we seemed to connect. I beckoned the kids to come over to the table and off she went. One hour passed, then two, and I began to panic. She'd said her name was Lisa, but I knew nothing else, and here I was at a table with five children acting like I was running a kid's camp with less than $3 to my name. Praying for wisdom, I carried on making the most of it all for the kids' sake.

Suddenly, in rushed Lisa. The relief of seeing her again bonded us together in inexplicable ways. She, too, knew only my name and had left her most precious children with me, a complete stranger. She was overjoyed to see us. She brought out a wad of money and announced that dinner was on her. The wave of relief I felt was immeasurable. She really didn't owe me anything, but we were starving. The kids ordered extravagantly, and we enjoyed each other's company and the food immensely. It was only when she asked if I would meet her there again the next day that I realized what was happening. She'd needed to "work the streets" to get enough money to get a place to stay, food to eat, and the necessities for her family. The realization that this woman had fed us while making such a risky, personal sacrifice felt sacred and painfully sad.

I had to make a choice. I could watch the kids while she worked or the other way around. I chose to watch the kids, first Lisa's kids, and then other moms' kids. We were all doing the best we could, but it didn't feel like the call of God.

An Old Story

A few days later, I was reminded of an old story: The rain had been relentless, and the waters were rising. A man prayed, "Lord, please save me from these flood waters." Just then, a small boat drifted past his door and a man called out to him to jump, offering to take him to safety. The homeowner sent the man in his boat away reassuring him that help was on the way.

As the water rose to the second story, the man was on his roof praying to the Lord, "Please save me from these flood waters." Just then, a helicopter hovered over his home, lowering a rope. The pilot called out for him to take hold so he could bring him to safety. The homeowner hollered back a thank you, but he was praying the Lord would save him from these flood waters, and the helicopter moved on. When the homeowner found himself in heaven, he asked with confusion, "Why didn't you answer my prayer?" The Lord responded, "I did. I sent you a boat and a helicopter, but you sent them away."

The Way Forward

I realized only then that the Lord had sent me the four men and their friends not only to provide housing for us, but also a community for my children. I see their broad, warm smiles in my mind's eyes today as I did then. They welcomed us as we returned, and I said yes. It was one of the best days of my life. The guys rearranged their things to make room for us. They built a three-story bunk bed for the kids and a friend donated a captain's bed with two built-in drawers under the mattress for me to use. We were safe, warm, and together. They gave us shelter and love, we gave them family and love.

We lived with these men for four years, and I never had to cook for them, clean for them, or sleep with them. They never asked for anything but gave of themselves to accommodate and care for us. They taught caring by example. They kept us safe and loved us. They helped as I finished my BA and started work on my master's degree. They helped me find employment, obtain legal immigration status, and eventually, vetted the man who was to become my new husband. We didn't necessarily look like it, but we were a true family.

In the course of time, I fell in love with my son's little league coach. The guys made it known that they were in my corner, and he was accountable to them. We married and he has been loving, honorable, caring, and respectful of all of us. We have been married for 28 years. We continue to see the guidance of the Holy Spirit in the patterns of our struggles and in our everyday lives. All along the voice of God has been there too. John, Jeff, Torger, Ryan and Michael, and the Holy Spirit, thank you!

Reflection:
- **Nancy had a dream in which she thought God was directing her to go to Seattle. Can you recall a time you felt that God was directing you toward something?**

- **Nancy left her home in the middle of the night to cross into the United States with little money, no passports, and no plan. This decision could have had a disastrous ending. Where do you see God's hand in her story? Where did people rise to the occasion to help her?**

- **Can you share a time a person unexpectedly helped you when you were in trouble or in a bad season in your life?**

Joe
Overcoming Addiction

Joe leads a small group called Digging Deeper that meets after the first service every Sunday to discuss the message and scriptures from that service. Joe, as a trained lay leader, leads the class. With his extensive knowledge of the Bible and a life of learning things the hard way, he can guide us to a deeper understanding of both the scriptures and the message our pastor had for us that day.

In our discussions, Joe often refers to his past addictions and struggles to break free of them. This is the tale of his journey out of the grip of alcohol and drugs into a relationship with God.

How I Was Saved

Growing up, we never attended church as a family. My parents would drop off my younger brother and me for Sunday School, and afterward, we would stay for the church service. In my early teens, I occasionally would usher during the worship service, but religion was not part of my family life.

My parents drank a lot, so when it was time to decide about drinking, I was all in. Alcohol, pot, LSD, mushrooms, and a lot of diet pills (amphetamines) were all part of my regular routine from the summer before my junior year in high school through college. Shortly after entering the workforce, I was introduced to cocaine.

Despite all of that, I managed to graduate from college, marry the girl of my dreams, have a daughter, and then three years later, a son. We didn't go to church; however, I felt God was looking out for me. Money was not a priority for us, and we decided we would live on whatever I earned and that my wife would be a stay-at-home mother. I felt God blessed that decision as I was wildly successful. By the time I was 29, I had checked all the boxes on my list of goals, but I was empty inside.

I remember December 13, 1983, very clearly. While driving home from work, I had a heart-to-heart talk with God and told Him there must be more to this life, and if He would show me what He wanted me to do, I would do it.

The next morning, I awoke with a hunger for the word of God. I found a Bible and started reading the book of Matthew. I believed Jesus was real, and I believed He rose from the dead, so I decided to start with His story. When I reached Matthew 11:28, and Jesus said, *"Come to me, all you who are weary and burdened, and I will give you rest,"* I knew I had to do more than believe there was a God. I had to give my life to Christ, and that's what I did.

For me that meant committing myself to learning the Bible, developing relationships with other Christians, and "walking the walk" as best I could. Drinking was still part of my life, but nothing like it had been, and in 1994, I quit drinking entirely. In addition to being a husband, a father, and a baseball coach, I became an officer in our church and a part-time preacher. It seemed like my life was good and right and just what I wanted, but I was focusing too much attention on work and activities outside the home, and I was setting myself up for a big shock.

In the spring of 1998, my wife informed me she didn't love me, hadn't loved me for years, and wanted a divorce. I just knew God wasn't going to let that happen; I had done everything I thought He had asked me to do for 14 years. I thought in my heart God hates divorce and He would ride in on a white horse and fix my marriage, but the divorce was final in December of 1999.

Soon after the divorce, I started drinking and taking drugs again and turned my back on God, on friends, and my family.

As it says in Galatians 6:1, *"God will not be mocked."* I felt God had stopped reaching out to me and had left me to my own destruction. At times, I heard Him call to me to return to Him, but for the most part, I ignored the call. He had not ridden in and fixed my problems even though I had done everything I thought He wanted. Looking back, I realize God was very patient and loving during those six years. He had kept me alive and out of jail while he was waiting for me to come back to Him.

After some time, I started attending a Baptist church. I had never been baptized as an adult, and I felt now was the time to wash away the sins of addiction and start anew. I invited my dad, kids, and friends to come to this important event in my life.

The night before my baptism, I called my drug dealer, and he delivered a large quantity of cocaine to my mailbox. I snuck out and got it and stayed up all night locked in my room by myself and did it all. I felt so dirty getting baptized after a night of cocaine that instead of getting a fresh start, I just kept using and carrying the guilt of that baptism for almost twenty years.

In the spring of 2004, I ended up in my first rehabilitation facility and met a lady who was 20 years younger than I was. She introduced me to heroin and other drugs, and we ended up leaving the facility together. Over the next eight or nine years, we both destroyed our lives, and I lost everything I had. I was lost in so many ways. God had not stepped in to fix my life like I wanted Him to do, and now I could do nothing but see myself as lost and unworthy.

Finally, my dad and stepmom came to North Carolina and took me back to their home in Florida. I had had enough. The Prodigal Son was ready to come home. God was with me. We were both at work to make me whole again.

I got back into the Word, back into church, and started going to Alcoholics Anonymous (AA) and Narcotics Anonymous (NA) meetings every day. It was a tremendous fight to break my addictions. There were many consequences in my physical, spiritual, and financial relationships, but God held my hand as I made my way on the journey.

My AA sponsor told me that pride was at the root of my problem, and as a result, I had never truly surrendered to God. He went on to explain to me that surrender did not mean you were losing the battle. Surrendering to God didn't make you a failure. He told me surrender means you don't have to fight anymore as God is now in charge, not you. It means living as Jesus taught us and letting God do the rest. I hugged my sponsor, held his hand, and for the first time in my life, surrendered.

On a Sunday soon after my surrender, my church in Florida was doing outdoor baptisms. My attention sharpened when it was Glen's turn to be baptized. Prior to moving to Florida, a tree had fallen on Glen doing irreparable damage to his body and brain. That freak accident caused him to lose everything: his career, his hobbies, his personality, and his relationships. Before the accident, he was a man of science, not of faith. Now there he was, struggling to get into the baptismal font. I moved forward, along with others, to help. I noticed the exertion and the determination on his face. He wanted this so much. I had never seen anyone work so hard to get baptized. He had lost everything he thought was important when that tree fell on him, but in losing everything, he had found God.

I had lost everything all those years ago, and my response was to numb myself with drugs. Tears of regret and shame were streaming down my face as I remembered my baptism from years ago. My body might have been present, but my mind and heart were numb from all the cocaine I had done the night before. That baptism had been a sham.

After moving forward to help Glen, I was left standing next to the senior pastor. I shared the story of my baptism and the guilt I still carried. He looked at me and said, "Go get changed, and let's baptize you today and fix that." And that's exactly what we did. The feeling of freedom was unbelievable!

What did I surrender to? I surrendered to the realization that Jesus Christ was indeed my Savior, but I had never made Him my Lord. Making Jesus my Lord and the most important part of my life meant that I was committed to learning His word as revealed in scripture. I also had the power of the Holy Spirit to apply that word to the way I was living my life. I could no longer hide behind drugs, anger, guilt, or ego.

There were times in my past when I chose to turn my back on God, but He was right there waiting for me, loving me, forgiving me. God's arms were open wide for me every time I clawed my way back. This last lonely, painful journey from addiction to a true commitment to Christ was so worth it. Now I know with all my being that God is in charge and loves me no matter how many times I left Him. Jesus is my Lord and my light, and He shows me how to live. And the Holy Spirit is guiding me to use my freedom and make my choices wisely and is providing me the power to live in this freedom.

Reflection:

- Joe often tells us in class to look at our checkbooks and our calendars to see what our priorities are. What is filling up your life?

- What do you do when you are faced with personal problems that seem overwhelming or unfair? What choices do you have?

- Joe says he hid behind drugs, anger, guilt, and ego. What do you hide behind?

- Were you baptized at an age when you made the decision and commitment for yourself? If so, how did you feel afterwards? Did you feel changed in any way?

Dwayne
From Crime to Christ, From Gangs to God, From Prison to Praise

If someone had told me ten years ago that one of my husband's best friends would be a 12-time felon, I would have dismissed the idea as preposterous. Yet here we are.

Dwayne is a radiantly joyful, larger-than-life black giant who runs a nonprofit for underprivileged kids in the worst neighborhood in Bradenton, Florida. He has three alter egos: He's "Bishop Freeze" when he's working in his nonprofit or doing ministry work; he's "DJ Freeze" when he is working his side hustle as a deejay; and he was "OG (Original Gangster) Freeze" in his youth and in prison.

When he moved to the Somerset section of Bradenton, Dwayne started walking around the neighborhood to check it out. He saw lots of kids in that neighborhood, and he also noticed there were drug dealers on every corner. Dwayne was working for Youth for Christ at the time and knew this created a bad atmosphere for the children in the area. So, he went up to each of the drug dealers and told them Somerset was now *his* neighborhood, and they needed to leave. When he told me that story, I asked him how the drug dealers responded to that. Dwayne laughed and said with a twinkle in his eye, "Well, they left. When I tell people to leave, they leave."

Since I was skeptical, he showed me some pictures of himself in prison. The photos showed Dwayne dressed in prison garb. He was younger and a bit rougher looking, but what really grabbed me was the eyes of the man in those pictures. The man looking out of those eyes was scary. Dangerous.

Someone who could hurt you. This was not the man sitting in the room with me. My friend Dwayne's eyes are full of light and love. This Dwayne was clearly a very different person from the man in the picture, and I was curious to hear the story of his transformation.

My Childhood

I don't ever remember my mother or father taking me to church, but my grandmother always made sure my siblings and I attended church with her every single Sunday. When I was nine years old, my mother married my stepfather, a young street hustler from Jamaica, and our lives changed forever. My stepfather enlisted in the army but soon went absent without leave. He took my mother, two sisters, two brothers, and me on a journey running from the law. We moved to Oklahoma City for a year; East Orange, New Jersey, for a year; and when I was 13, to Tacoma, Washington, where his criminal lifestyle reached a new high.

I still had a desire to attend church, so once we settled in Tacoma, my mother found a local church to attend, and every Sunday morning my siblings and I would go to Sunday school and children's church. It gave me peace and made me feel safe. I really liked being around Christian people who seemed to care for me, because at home I frequently witnessed my stepfather beating my mother in moments of rage, and I took quite a few beatings myself. Whenever I would get in trouble at home or at school, my stepfather would grab me by the neck and hold me up against the wall with my feet off the ground, then suddenly let me fall. Before I hit the floor, he would punch me in my stomach knocking the wind out of me. I was terrified of this man, but whenever I went to church, I felt safe. As long as I was there and away from my stepfather, I felt I was in good hands. I would pray to Jesus and ask him to help me get my family away from this crazy man.

Beginning a Life of Crime

When I was twelve, my stepfather started involving me in his criminal lifestyle. We would take the subway to Harlem, New York. He would make me hold a brown paper bag with different colored balloons in it, saying, "I want you to stand across the street and hold this bag in your coat. Play with your basketball, but when I call out a color, I want you to reach in the bag and pull out that color balloon. When somebody walks up to you, give it to them." Before long I figured out what was in those balloons…it was heroine. My stepfather was teaching me how to sell drugs before I was even a teenager.

Around this same time, my stepfather decided we weren't going to Sunday school anymore. He would take my eldest brother and me to various neighborhoods, and we would burglarize people's homes while they were in church. I kept praying for God to get this man out of our lives. This was not who I wanted to be.

One night I thought I was dreaming when I heard my stepfather say, "Get up right now! Come down in the basement with me." I couldn't believe it when I saw he had handcuffs on. Handcuffs! Had he been arrested? I very much hoped so. He told me to grab a hacksaw and try to saw off one of the handcuffs. I worked on those handcuffs for the next two hours, wishing the whole time that they would never come off. I finally got one arm free, and he let me go back to bed. To my great relief, the police came to the house the next morning and took him into custody. I was so glad he was finally in jail. Our whole family breathed easier.

The Damage was Done

By the time I was 15 years old, my stepfather was serving time in prison, and my mother could not control me. During the last few years, I had built up a lot of anger. You would think I would start going to Sunday School again now that my stepfather was gone, but the past three years had put church and Jesus in my rearview mirror, and they were no longer priorities. I embraced the culture of "the hood."

There was never enough food in our house. I started shoplifting food, smoking weed, and bullying everyone in my neighborhood. I ended up in juvenile hall numerous times for numerous crimes. I eventually was sentenced to 32 weeks in a juvenile detention camp for stealing a car to go joyriding.

By the time I was 21 years old, my friends and I had run into trouble with a street gang called the LA Cribs, so I decided to start my own gang. I also decided if I was going to be in a gang, I was going to be the leader. We called ourselves the Hilltop Bloods, and my new name was O.G. Freeze, O.G. for Original Gangster. Yes, I was now a gangster, and before long, I was indicted by the Feds for gang racketeering, distribution of crack cocaine, and federal felony firearm charges.

"God, please help me get out of this situation." It seemed like every time I got in trouble, I always found myself praying for God's help. At that time, God was only someone I looked to when I needed help, but help wasn't coming. I took a plea bargain for a 10-year prison sentence because I knew if I went to trial, I would likely be sentenced to at least 30 years behind bars. I was 22 years old with a 10-year federal prison sentence and felt like I was cornered by my life's obstacles, powerless to resist, and my destiny was failure.

Life in Prison

To survive in prison with my gang status, I had to join the prison Bloods immediately. Their leader gave me a homemade knife and said, "Hide this in your cell and when it's time for war, get your knife and go stab our enemies." I was on the wrong path with the wrong people, but I saw no other way to survive.

Before long, one of our gang members was assaulted and stabbed in the neck with an ice pick and almost died. We Bloods had to retaliate, and a major prison riot broke out. After the riot was over, our entire gang was locked up in solitary confinement. While I was in solitary confinement, I got word my sister had died and requested permission to go to the funeral. When the request was denied, I lost all control and, in my grief and fury, I beat up all four guards who came to subdue me.

For my participation in the riot and for beating up the guards, the warden arranged for me to be sent to the Marion Illinois Supermax Prison where I would be locked in a cell 23 hours a day. I was now considered one of America's most dangerous inmates. The Marion Supermax became the United States' highest security prison by 1978 and was the holding place for the Federal Bureau of Prisons' most dangerous prisoners. Even though I was 6'3", 250 pounds with 22" biceps, when we pulled up to the prison and I saw the razor wire and armed guards, I was afraid. I began to pray again. "Lord, please help me. Please keep me safe."

Temporarily out of Prison

When I was 30 years old, I was released from federal prison. When I returned to my neighborhood in Tacoma, I was now respected and feared as an original gangster who survived death and prison and was free again to lead the Bloods. I felt trapped and cornered, powerless to resist, and headed for failure once again. It seemed like everywhere I went I was surrounded by gangs, drugs, crime, and violence. Whenever my gang members came around, I would always end up committing crimes and engaging in violence. I had no power to resist the evil temptations. Either I was going to be murdered, or I was going to end up back in prison.

To no one's surprise, I was arrested when I was 33, this time for felony assault. Now I was facing the three strikes rule that carries a minimum prison sentence of life without the possibility of parole. As I was awaiting my trial date, I felt hopeless and thought my life was over.

Jesus Shows Up in Jail

While I was in jail awaiting trial, a correction officer came by and asked if anyone wanted to go to the jail church service. Gangsters like me didn't go to church in jail because it was viewed as a sign of weakness. But for some reason, I didn't care what anyone thought of me. Something inside was pulling me to go to church, and nothing was going to stop me.

The message that day was, "Jesus loves you and no matter what you've done, he will forgive you. No sins are too great for his grace. If you confess your sins, he will forgive you and cleanse you from all unrighteousness." As the prison preacher shared his message, those words were so powerful they spoke directly to my heart. I started to remember when I was a young boy going to church with my grandmother, and I felt goosebumps all over my body as tears started to roll down my face. I could be forgiven. I could be loved in spite of everything I'd done.

When I got back to my cell, I got on my knees and began to pray, "Lord, I'm so sorry for all the wrong I've done. I believe you are the Son of God, Jesus, and I believe you died for my sins. Forgive me. I don't want to be a gangster anymore. I'm tired of spending my life in prison. Lord, if you can forgive me and change me, I promise I will never lead a gang again. Lord, even if I have to spend the rest of my life in prison, I will serve you if you change me."

I cried out to the Lord in my cell for what seemed like all night, and I felt the spirit of God in that room with me. I heard a small voice speak to me and tell me I was forgiven, *"I love you, Dwayne. You are my son. You are a new man."* All I could say was, "Thank you. Lord, thank you, Lord, thank you, Father." I'll never forget that day in October of 2000. The God of grace and mercy saved me, delivered me, and set me free from the bondage of sin.

As I continued to wait for my trial date, I started a Bible study in jail, went to church regularly, and my lifestyle as an inmate radically changed. The Lord performed a true miracle in my case. The prosecutor recognized the change in me and decided to offer me a plea bargain for three more years in prison instead of a life sentence. Hallelujah! I remembered the scripture of Isaiah 61:1: "The Spirit of the Lord GOD is on me because the LORD has anointed me to preach good news to the poor. He has sent me to bind up the brokenhearted, to proclaim liberty to the captives and freedom to the prisoners." God's Word was being fulfilled in my life.

The endless cycle of sin, crime, gangs, and violence had finally been broken. Three years later, I was released from prison and was finally free at last.

"So if the Son sets you free, you will be free indeed." – John 8:36

I no longer felt trapped or cornered now that I had the power of God to resist evil temptations. My destiny turned from failure to prosperity, success, and eternal glory. After I was released, the Lord called me to join a ministry called Youth for Christ in Tacoma, Washington, where I was blessed to be able to serve as a juvenile chaplain. The odds of me ever becoming a juvenile chaplain and getting clearance to go back behind the walls to speak God's word to juvenile inmates were minimal at best - and was a miracle in itself.

One day I felt a call to move back to my birthplace of Bradenton, Florida. Because the spirit of God was flowing through me vigorously, I answered that call, moved to Bradenton, and began working for Youth for Christ there and later started my own nonprofit for kids in one of the lowest income neighborhoods in the county.

Because of my life experiences, I know the challenges and temptations underprivileged kids and teens are facing every day. I know how easy it is to fall into a life of crime when you're hungry, when you're hanging around the wrong people, or when a life of crime is all you know. I am determined to break the cycle of crime and desperation for as many young people as possible.

Ten years after I moved to Bradenton, I was ordained as a pastor. Who would have ever thought I would be called to become a pastor? I have truly gone from crime to Christ, from gangs to God, and from prison to praise. Hallelujah!

Reflection:

- If you had a parent or adult in your life who was abusive or pulling you into a life you didn't want, how did you break free of this person?

- For a long time, Dwayne's relationship with God just consisted of him asking God for help. What does a good relationship with God look like?

- Dwayne saw nothing but obstacles in his way but didn't see that his biggest obstacle was his perceived belief that he had no choice but to live a life of crime. What do we need to do when we are desperate for a change, but can't see how to make it happen?

Lyndzey
A Transformed Life

Lyndzey is a force of nature. I'm 5'10". She's taller, and you can literally feel her strength just standing next to her. She has a wide, bright smile, a strong faith, and exudes confidence from every pore. It wasn't always so. Lyndzey grew up in my hometown of Eden, NC, but she and I had drastically different experiences. She always loved her mother, but she and her sister did not always feel safe in their own house because of the men in her mother's life. Here is her story.

A Tough Beginning

My mother got pregnant with me when she was just 15 years old. My father was 16. They were young and in love, so they got married and became parents before they were out of high school. I will always be grateful to her for choosing to risk her life and her future to bring me into the world. When she was 17, she got pregnant with my sister. At 18 years old, my mom had two children and the world on her shoulders.

My father reacted to having a wife and two children by the age of 19 by becoming an alcoholic who was extremely volatile and abusive. To save herself and her children, my mom had to escape from my father and begin her life as a full-time single parent. Growing up with just my mom didn't seem abnormal to me. My mother always found a way to put food on the table, clothes on our backs, and a roof over our heads. We might not have had a lot, but my sister and I felt safe and loved.

Then my mom began to date a lot of different men. I felt uneasy because I had a bitter taste in my mouth about men in general. Based on my experience during the few years I had lived on earth, men weren't trustworthy. They were mean and abusive, and honestly, I had no use for them in my life.

47

Then my mother remarried when I was about seven years old. I liked my stepdad. He wasn't abusive and there wasn't much arguing. My baby brother was born, and life seemed to settle down for me. But this relationship didn't last, and a few years later, they divorced. I did not understand why but that was just the way it was. I was 11 years old and now living with a single parent again.

My mom worked so hard to provide for us while my siblings and I were growing up. She was a waitress for most of my life and picked up jobs on the side here and there to pay the rent and keep food on the table. I could tell she was sad, and that something was missing in her life.

My mother was never without a man in her life for long. She started to date this one guy soon after her divorce, and I did not like him at all. He was just like all the others.

By the time I was in middle school, I had discovered my God-given talent for sports. I loved sports, particularly softball and volleyball, and I was good at both. My sister and I played on school sports teams and in the YMCA leagues every season. Not only did we love playing, but being on teams meant after-school practice and that meant I wouldn't have to go home right after school to see my mom being mistreated. For the next few years, sports were my outlet and my escape from reality.

In the summer before my ninth-grade year, the CEO of the YMCA came up to us right after a softball game. We had heard some rumors he was getting divorced and was mean and kind of weird, but I tried not to think about those things. He introduced himself as Barry and asked us if we would like to help out at the concession stands. He promised us free food, so we agreed to help and worked until late at night. He took all the volunteers out to dinner that night, and I observed most of the rumors I heard didn't seem true at all. Barry seemed funny, nice, and caring. I still had concerns, and my walls were up because my experience with men had always been bad. But Barry seemed different.

The softball tournament lasted a week, and my sister and I continued to play and volunteer afterwards at the concession stand. Every day we would play our tournament games and volunteer afterwards. Barry took the umpires and the volunteers out to dinner every night, and I got to know him much better. That week I determined that the rumors that he was mean were simply not true. I had never known a man like Barry. When the tournament was over, my mom dropped us off at the Y while she worked. I wanted to express my gratitude to Barry for being so nice to us and paying for our dinner for a week, so we went straight to his office to thank him and tell him we were interested in more volunteer work. He walked us to the childcare room to help take care of the kids and went back to his office.

That day, when he left to go to lunch, he began to wonder if my sister and I had anything to eat and turned around and came back to invite us to go to lunch with him. In the car, I began to worry that my sister and I were now alone with this man. What if the rumors were true? We were taking a risk. What if he was acting nice, but had bad intentions? My walls were still up, and I was alert for any signs that things were going to go wrong. When we got our lunch, Barry prayed for the meal. We prayed at home, but that was the first time I had ever seen a man initiate a prayer.

When we were with Barry, our conversations were light, upbeat, and full of humor. It was easy being with Barry. He reminded me of my great-grandfather. My sister and I continued to volunteer at the Y, and Barry would take us to lunch. My mom had some concerns. She had also heard the rumors he was mean and wasn't sure we should be spending so much time with a man going through a divorce. I later found out he was also being cautioned that we might try to take advantage of him.

After a month of this routine, I remember one lunch in particular. We were at a pizza buffet. While Barry was fixing his plate, my sister and I were sitting at the table waiting for him. A question popped into my head. I turned to my sister and asked her if she would want Barry to take care of us if something happened to our mom. She replied, "Do you think something is going to happen to Mom?" I told her I didn't think so, but if it did, would she trust Barry to take care of us. She said yes. I don't know why that question popped into my head, and I don't know why I thought we couldn't go to our grandparents or other family members. But the thing is, I had a strong feeling I wanted to ask Barry to take care of us.

When Barry came back to the table with his plate full, we prayed over our food. Then I stared at him, wondering how I could ask this huge question. He noticed me staring and said, "What is it?" Then I asked him if he would take care of us if something ever happened to our mom. He replied, "Lyndzey, nothing is going to happen to your mom. I'm not very good at math, but I'm 54 and your mom is 30, so if anything is going to happen to anybody, it will be me."

I said, "I know, Barry, but if something *does* happen to my mom, would you take care of us?" He said, "I've seen the way you guys work in the concession stand. You have a lot of friends. You have family. Someone will help you out."

I wasn't getting the answer I wanted, so with more determination, I asked him one last time, "If something happens to our mom, we want YOU to take care of us. Will you take care of us?" Out of desperation that his food was getting cold, he said yes, but added that nothing was going to happen to our mom. After that affirmation, my walls finally went down with him.

Both of Barry's children had gone on to play collegiate tennis. I was about to start my ninth-grade year and knew if I wanted a volleyball scholarship, I needed to begin preparing, and thought Barry might be the best person to advise me on how to get that scholarship. When I expressed this desire to him, he gave me a reality check when he said, "Well, you're behind." With a serious expression, he explained that I would have to work very hard to get there, but if I was serious about this, he would pick me up at 5:00 am every morning to work out before school, and then we would work out again after school. In addition, I would have to qualify for a traveling volleyball team.

I agreed to all of this, so we worked out before and after school. Finally, I was ready for an official tryout in the closest city. There were about 150 girls trying out. I felt so small that day. All I could do was try my best. To my surprise, I made the team. Not only did Barry pay for my club fees and travel expenses, but he also took me to every practice and to every tournament. Our relationship continued to grow. In my mind, Barry fluctuated from being a grandfather figure to a father figure to a friend.

As the volleyball season of my junior year approached, Barry took me to our capital city to try out for the top girls' volleyball team in the state. This time there were 100 girls trying out for my division. I was so nervous! Barry told me to get noticed. He said to take the first ball that came to me and hit it as hard as I could. He said to try to hit the scoreboard on the far wall or hit the ceiling. Just get noticed. I didn't do that, but I played as well as I could and made the team. That was the first time in my life I didn't feel small. I felt I wasn't behind anymore. I could make something out of myself. But there was a problem. The cost to join this team was $8,800, a fee that covered all the costs of travel. My mother didn't have that kind of money.

Barry not only paid the fee, but he drove me an hour and a half to practice three days a week. The drive plus the two-hour practice consumed five hours of both our days. While I was making a commitment to myself and my future, Barry was making a commitment to me.

I realized this was the first time I could believe what a male said was true. I finally had a man in my life I could trust and depend on. Everything in the world seemed right.

A few months after I made the team, I was working out in Barry's basement when he received a phone call from my grandmother. She was on the speakerphone so I could hear her plainly. Her voice was worried and frantic as she informed us my mom was in a terrible car accident. It was unclear as to how bad it was, but she was already in the ICU. I remember the silence between Barry and me, but as we walked to his car, I asked him if he remembered what he promised at the pizza place. He replied, "Honey, I've already thought about that," and we headed to the hospital.

Many thoughts raced through my head. Was this real? Could this really be happening? Once we got to the hospital, I found my whole family was already there. Only the immediate family could go back to see her, and then for only five minutes. She was in a coma and needed brain surgery among many other treatments. It was very possible she might not live, so this was our chance to say goodbye.

When I went into the ICU to see her, that's when I first felt anger toward God. If God was real, where was He? Whether He was real or not, He had certainly gotten my attention. Unlimited emotions welled up in me as I saw how damaged her body was with her head dented in and bones sticking out of her. I didn't care about volleyball or school or anything else in this world. I just wanted my mom not to be in this horrific condition. My mother had always had such a hard life. She had had so much pain and abuse; she didn't deserve this.

My mother was going to need care for the rest of her life, whether it be long or short. My sister and I moved in with Barry, but shortly after, he decided to move to West Palm Beach to be near his daughter. I was going to go wherever Barry went, but my sister decided it would be best if she went to live with our great-aunt. I moved with Barry, and he officially became my legal guardian.

That summer, I got invited to go on a volleyball missions' trip to Costa Rica. Truthfully, I didn't care about the God part at that time. I just wanted to go to another country and play volleyball. I was quickly humbled by God during this week-long trip and finally started to see the bigger picture. After observing so much suffering in this third-world country, God reminded me of all the blessings that I have. I have come to realize that ultimately all things work together for His good and His purpose. I had to believe and trust God was going to use the situation with my mom, this horrible situation, for good.

After high school, I got a volleyball scholarship to Palm Beach Atlantic. While in college, I got involved with the kind of man my mother was always attracted to. He and I had a chaotic relationship, and I stepped away from the Christian ways Barry had taught me. At some point, Barry told me he didn't approve of the choices I was making, and I needed to decide if I wanted to live a Christian life or be a party girl. I chose the latter. Barry looked at me and said, "We've been down this road before with this guy, and if you chose him again, I'm not going to be part of it." That man had a spell on me, so I packed my things and left.

Finally, on one of the many days that man made me cry, I came to my senses and realized I was just repeating all the mistakes my mother had made, and her mother had made before her. I called Barry and asked if he would take me back. He said yes, but I had to change my ways. I came back to Barry and back to God and left all that chaos and drama behind. I put my energy into my church, my schoolwork, and my volleyball teams.

Nine years after my mom's car accident, she is still alive, but has limited abilities and is under constant care.

Even with all that, I am thankful for God's grace for keeping her alive. Today I am working at a Christian school as an assistant athletic director, and best of all, I am married to the gentlest, serving, God-fearing man I know.

Reflection:

- **Lyndzey was born into a family where the women started to have babies in their mid-teens and were drawn to men who did not have models of how to be good husbands and fathers. What have been the generational patterns in your family?**

Barry
A Fatherless Child

In Lyndzey's story, she said that she heard rumors at the YMCA that Barry was weird. Jim and I have known him for a long time. I wouldn't call him weird, but he is the only man I have ever met who would take in two teenagers and put the amount of time, money, and energy to turn one of them into a volleyball phenom. Now that Lyndzey is grown and married, Barry is homeschooling his twin grandsons and training them in tennis. He doesn't stop at academics and sports. Barry teaches and guides any youngsters who are in his care into a Christian lifestyle and provides them with the skills to be successful as adults. What he does with kids is amazing. Here is why he does it.

A Surrogate Father

My father left my mother and me when I was young. There were a great many boys in my hometown who grew up without a father figure, and I would have been one of them had it not been for three men who stepped in to teach, guide, and advise me, all of whom I met through church.

After my father left, my mom became the breadwinner of our house. My maternal grandmother lived with us and had to have a caregiver because of her Alzheimer's. To make ends meet, my mom worked three jobs, six days a week. She worked from 3:00 pm to 11:00 pm at the local mill on weekdays, so she went to work at the exact time I got out of school. I could have gone home and stayed with my grandmother and her caregiver, but as a young boy with a lot of energy and a love for sports, I wanted to be outside playing with other kids.

My Sunday School teacher at the Osborne Baptist Church lived in my neighborhood. He spent a lot of time with me playing games and was the coach of my baseball team when I was a little older. Like many other neighborhood kids, I went over to his house after school every day to hang out and play basketball in his backyard.

I remember one afternoon when we were playing basketball, I went up for a shot at the basket and when it missed, I called a foul. Hilton said, "No Barry, you weren't fouled." I believed I had indeed been fouled, so I got mad. He was supposed to be on my side. With my feelings hurt, I went inside and decided to take my chess set and go home. I wasn't going to stick around someone who wouldn't take my side. I grabbed my chess set and walked out the door. By the time I got to the end of the sidewalk, I had changed my mind. Hmmm, but how was I going to fix this? It had already gotten dark, so I decided to drop my chess set and let all the pieces fall out on the ground. Then I'd go back and ask Hilton for a flashlight to find the pieces. I knew he would come outside to help me; then he would make everything all right. It went according to plan, except one of my chessmen got broken when it fell. Many years later, I came across the chess set and looked inside and noticed the broken pieces. I made a little wooden base and glued the two broken pieces to it. To this day, I have that broken chess piece on the bookshelf in my condo to remind me of Hilton.

After I got out of college, I took Hilton to lunch. I told him I would never be able to thank him for what he had done for me as a child. I said, "I feel like I ought to buy you a car or something, but I don't have the money to do that." He told me he didn't need a new car, but there was a way I could repay him. Hilton said, "One day you will meet a kid who will need your help. When you help him, you will have paid ole Hilton back." I tucked that thought in my head and went on with my life.

Some years later, when the YMCA in our town needed a new CEO, my other two mentors recommended the YMCA Board hire me. That recommendation went a long way toward my getting that job. The Y had always been an integral part of my life. During my school years, I had always been in and out of the Y as a member and volunteer. When I went to work there, it felt like my second home. I served as the CEO there for 28 years.

It turns out that if you work at a YMCA, all you have to do is open your eyes to find a child who needs your help. While I was there, so many of them lacked a father figure and wondered every day if they would have enough to eat. That's why I started taking my volunteers out to dinner every night. Knowing what it was like not to have a father around, I helped as many kids as I could as problems arose.

Then one night Lyndzey's mother was in a horrific accident, and I knew I needed to step up and do what God wanted me to do. I had made Lyndzey and her sister a promise I never thought I would have to keep. My son and daughter from my broken marriage were living with me, but we all found a place to sleep in my three-bedroom home. Honoring my promise to take care of Lyndzey and her sister has given me great joy and added a second daughter to my family.

I guess I have paid ole Hilton back.

Reflection:

- **What was your experience with your own father?**

- **Were there other men in your life who served as father figures or role models? Who were they?**

- **How is Barry's story of Hilton and the chess set a parable of how we can interact with God?**

Sylvia
Loss

Every small town has people who are well regarded for their work to make the town a better place for all. Sylvia and Johnny were two such people. When Johnny died of melanoma in 2013 at the age of 78, the town turned out in full force with the walls of the church lined by the entire police department who wanted to honor their mayor.

Sylvia is a small woman with a big smile. Even though she is now in her late 80s, she still exudes the same positive energy she's always had meeting everyone with a warm smile and a cheerful greeting. Most of the members of our Bible study group at the Methodist Church knew her as the mayor's wife, a mother of two, a hospital recruiter, a church trustee, and a community volunteer. They also knew her as a person who was quicker to share her blessings than her grievances, and that Johnny also had that same trait as well.

The minister of the church was our group leader, and when we finished studying the Book of Lamentations, he invited us to write a lamentation and share it with the group. At our next meeting, he asked if anyone wanted to read their lamentation, and Sylvia immediately volunteered. As she began to read, the room quickly stilled. We had no idea this cheerful, unfailingly positive woman carried so much pain.

Sylvia's Lament

Oh God, who has taken away my children We prayed. Where were you?
I yearn to see their grownup faces, To hear their grownup voices,
To share their children.

You blessed us, Oh God, by sparing one Sending one
And for those two I praise you
But in the night when darkness covers me

I weep for the three whom I no longer know…

Who are still small children in my mind.
And I wonder still… We prayed.
Where were you?

For now…we see through a glass darkly.

Needless to say, the group had questions. Sylvia's husband Johnny was my husband's uncle, and he told me they had lost three children, his cousins, to a rare genetic disorder in the 1960s before they moved to our town, but he said it so matter-of-factly that I failed to grasp the enormity of those words.

Sylvia shared the basic facts with the group that day, but I was curious to learn more. It would be ten years later before I got to hear the whole story. The pandemic gave Sylvia the silence and the time to go up to her attic and bring down the boxes she packed with each child's pictures and mementos after they died. The memories came flooding back, and she decided to write a book detailing what happened so their story would not be lost.

This story of resilience and survival really belongs to both Sylvia and Johnny because they went through this tragic experience side by side, but it is told from Sylvia's point of view.

My Story

Johnny Grogan and I were married in the Church of the Epiphany in Eden on December 19, 1959. Our first child, Marcia, was born on December 19, a year later. She was beautiful and became our total life. Our second child, Jay, was born June 25, 1964. We were excited to have a son. He looked like his dad.

Oh, the joy of having children! We made our flat backyard into a neighborhood kids' playground with swings and slides and a merry-go-round. There were a lot of kids on our street, and it was a great place to be for Marcia, Jay, and all their friends. There was energy and joy all around.

On the morning of December 15,1965, Marcia said she had a "hurtness" in her arms and then in her legs. Instinctively, Johnny and I rushed her to our doctor. He wasn't sure what was wrong and admitted her to the local hospital for tests. She was in constant pain when she was touched.

She died 16 hours after her first complaint. Even with an autopsy, there was no explanation.

Beautiful flowers filled our house. But when all the "funeral flowers" began to die, the reality of death permeated our home. I vividly remember the extreme sadness and grief of throwing out the flowers when they died. Oh, the symbolic finality of that simple act!

Johnny shut down, and I needed to talk. I needed to explain what I was feeling. I had questions and needed answers. Our minister, Roger Westmoreland, spent hours helping me face what was happening as I tried to cope with the unbelievable grief over the death of my beautiful child.

Roger had lost a child too, so we were able to talk parent to parent. I would have lost my mind with grief if it hadn't been for Roger's presence. I walked with Roger and talked and questioned. We prayed. I prayed to make it through the day and to understand. God was in this story somewhere I felt. But I felt so lost and separated. All I could think about was Marcia. I remember praying to die so I could be with her. I read books on grief. I read about Jesus and the Easter story. I tried to understand life after death. How did all this relate to what happened to my Marcia?

Our friends surrounded us with love. Johnny and I began to talk and love one another even more. Our community grieved with us. I learned to forgive people for what they said or did that hurt me as I grieved. But I was still lost inside.

In the midst of all this sadness, I discovered I was pregnant again. I was excited to have this new life growing within me. On June 6, 1967, Kevin was born to us. He was a beautiful white-haired child. He actually looked like Marcia, while Jay was growing to be a "little Johnny." He had a Superman cape he wanted to wear day and night, and we found that so endearing. I began to feel as if I could make it emotionally and mentally. There was a rhythm to our lives.

Then, on a June morning in 1968, Jay complained of pains eerily similar to Marcia's. Even Jay was rattled by the similarities and wanted to know if he was "going up there where Marcia was." Our doctor sent us to the ER of a bigger hospital in a larger community. Jay, dressed in his usual Superman cape, was put in a medical tent to help him breathe. We were panic-stricken. We discovered he was, indeed, fighting the same disease as Marcia with different symptoms. The muscles in Jay's throat were affected, and he had a hard time swallowing. The possibility of death crept in with the fear.

The doctors told us they thought they discovered a pattern. This child-killer had a name, Intermittent Hemo- myoglobinuria. With only 20 reported cases of myoglobinuria from which to compare details, the doctors started treating Jay with a simple bicarbonate of soda mixture as directed by the literature. It was given intravenously. Within days, Jay's throat was improving. He began to swallow. He even ate his favorite cereal – Cheerios. In four days, he was discharged with great celebration. The doctors felt the condition was probably no longer an issue for him.

In November, we happily went to be with family for Thanksgiving. Jay came to our bed one early morning and was talking to us in silly-speak. I told him to talk so I could understand him, and then I realized his throat was being attacked. There it was again! We headed for the ER while our doctor called in orders. The next hours were agonizing. The ER doctors told us Jay was not sick. He referred us to a local pediatrician. All the while, Jay's condition was deteriorating, and we were panicking, trying to explain the unexplainable to anyone who would listen. Finally, someone called an ambulance that took Jay back to the hospital with the pediatrician sitting beside our son.

The doctors examined Jay and reported he was doing well. He encouraged us to go downstairs for a cup of coffee. With a sigh of relief, we did. Before the coffee could be served, we were paged to come back to the pediatric floor. Jay had died. Only six hours had passed since he had come to our bed. It was November 30, 1969, and Jay was five years old.

Again, we were living with the death of a child, our second death. Roger Westmoreland once again was responsible for the funeral. Jay was buried beside Marcia. The son who was so like Johnny was gone. This time, I could not bear to go to the cemetery. I grieved at home. I really felt Roger had said everything when Marcia died, so what was left for me to hear or to learn?

Amidst all the emotional upheaval with Jay, I learned I was pregnant again. The joy was missing as we discussed whether to have the baby knowing our medical history. We made our decision to end the pregnancy and scheduled an abortion.

I told my dad, and he cried. He pleaded with me to have the child. I called Johnny and we drove back to talk to our doctor again. His reaction was, "If you have a child, and the child lives three or four years, you will have had the joy of that child for that time. We just do not know about the illness, though."

Johnny and I went back home determined to have this baby and love it for however long. Meredith was born on Easter weekend, April 5, 1969. We were so happy and felt we had made the right decision.

In August 1970, when Kevin was three, I noticed he was dragging a leg. I called our doctor and took Kevin to be seen. The doctor said it "could" be the same condition but was not sure. He arranged for Kevin and me to go to Duke University Hospital to work with a doctor named Dr. James Sidbury whose specialty was muscle diseases including myoglobinuria.

Dr. Sidbury was honest and told us this was new to him. He had never seen death in patients with this disease and labeled it "familial myoglobinuria." Kevin was returned to his room after testing, He woke up listless. I helped him go to the bathroom and saw his urine was very dark. Dr. Sidbury came back and verified Kevin was in the middle of an attack. The staff started the same procedure that had been done before. Kevin lived through the night and was discharged three days later.

The morning after Christmas, that same year, Kevin came into our bedroom and said he did not feel well. I made a pallet for him in the den and covered him up. A little later, he came back into our room, and we thought he looked paler and wondered if he might be in the middle of an attack. We called the doctor and met him in the Emergency. Kevin's heart muscle had been attacked and he had had a heart attack! He died within four hours of his not feeling well. He was three years old.

Roger Westmoreland preached the funeral at the cemetery in the rain. He ended by saying "And now we see through a glass darkly." Soon after Kevin's funeral, this beloved minister and friend died of a heart attack himself. The very air we breathed felt as if it had disappeared. The one person who had walked with us through our grief was now gone also.

Recovery

It was hard to separate "us" from the "tragedy of us." Our church surrounded us with love as best they could. It was such a sad time. The people there felt our pain so deeply, but they and we couldn't move forward. Death was defining us and our relationships. It was not healthy for any of us! We were always 'seeing through the glass darkly". During a children's event one Sunday, it all became clear. We had to leave the love we felt in this church in order to find our love of life again.

I began to think about adopting a child and Johnny was open to the idea. We decided to try to adopt an older child, preferably a boy. I called the Children's Home Society to make an appointment. The person began gathering information about our family. She listened to our history and our story and finally said, "We do not give parents children; we give children good homes." She said because of all our trauma, we could not offer a stable environment at that moment. She was probably right, but I was disappointed.

Johnny had a good friend who was the Director of the Department of Social Services. He suggested we meet with the adoption counselor. We did and were so impressed that we decided to take her advice and just see what happened. Sure enough, after visiting several children on daycare playgrounds, we decided maybe adoption was not for us. Thank goodness, Johnny and I both felt the same. We told the counselor not to go any further in the process.

But later, she did call. She began by telling us about a child who had just been released for adoption. He was three, and his name was Michael. His name was Michael!

Meredith had an imaginary friend named Michael! We met him at the Sears Toyland and when Johnny picked him up, Michael started talking and they bonded. A prolific talker at age three, we wanted to take him home that night. It definitely felt like it was meant to be.

Meredith totally accepted her new brother in our home. I worried because suddenly all the attention of our friends would be on Michael, but it didn't seem to bother Meredith. She had a strong personality and was totally accepting. She was so dear and seemed truly to be excited for him to be with us. Meredith and Michael even looked like twins, although they were six months apart in age.

When Meredith had her sixth birthday, we felt in our hearts she was safe. I remember packing away clothes for Meredith and feeling comfortable they would be worn again. We began to relax. We felt Meredith was going to be okay, and, for the first time, I felt we were all going to be okay. Healing love was finding its way back into our lives.

Johnny and I lived many years with the incredible impact of trauma in our lives. Three of our beloved children had died of a genetic condition. We had to learn the fine art of cohabitating with death without letting it destroy us or our faith. Many marriages cannot survive the death of a single child, much less three, but I had Johnny. He was my hand holder, my hugger, my steadfast protector who was there – side by side as we held each other up and lived it all together…each of us making it possible for the other to survive.

Neither one of us ever blamed God, but we struggled to understand the path He had in mind for us. We didn't always understand the "why," but we always recognized the blessings of the Holy Spirit during each heartbreak: Roger Westmoreland and his understanding words; our dear friends who surrounded us with love; our church community who kept us tethered; Meredith, the child who lived; Michael, who completed our family; my dad, who convinced us to choose life over fear; and the many professionals along the way. So many people shared God's love and support with us. Because of them, even when our grief was overwhelming, the voice of the Holy Spirit was stronger.

Now that I am in my eighties and recall the overwhelming sadness of our loss, and our ability to survive it intact, I realize Johnny and I must have been cradled in the lap of God.

And I am still there.

Reflection:

- Sylvia wondered where God was while she was dealing with the loss of one child after another.

- When have you wondered where God was in your life?

- Where can you find the hand of God in Sylvia's story?

- Do you find it easier to see God at work in other people's lives than your own? Reflect on your life and see where the God moments were or where a person or opportunity showed up just when you needed it.

Zack

Born to be Wild; Saved by Two Fathers

Zack is a big guy with a big smile and a big personality. He made some bad choices in his life, which landed him in prison for many years. He now owns a tile business and in his off hours, he gives inspirational talks to groups of both adults and young people. My husband heard him speak at his men's group and came home telling me I needed to hear Zack's story. We hired him to seal the tile in our bathrooms, and while he was on his hands and knees on my floor, I asked him about his story. He told me he had one of his talks on a flash drive and another on his Facebook page. He gave me the flash drive, and with that and his Facebook page, I put together his story.

As with all the stories in this book, once the story was in readable form, I sat down with Zack to make sure I had written a fair and accurate representation of his story. When he got to the end, he gasped and visibly flinched as if he had been punched in the stomach. After watching his video on Facebook, I read every single comment that other viewers had made. Comments on Facebook are listed with the most recent at the top, so it wasn't until I got to the first few comments that I found a treasure Zack had never seen.

Wild Child

Growing up in Florida, I was a wild child. Nothing but trouble. It wasn't because of bad parenting; I just would not listen when my mom and stepdad tried to teach me right from wrong. My first encounter with the law was for shoplifting at the age of five. I caused trouble in school, at home, and everywhere I went. I started smoking weed at 13, and by the age of 16, I was a full-fledged criminal, in and out of juvenile court for stealing and doing drugs.

At age 18, I went to prison for a year for stealing a car. I was out for only three months before I was sent back for manufacturing meth. When I was released the second time, my dad offered to include me as part of his work and his family. My dad had never been a part of my life, so I accepted his invitation and started working for him, traveling around the country and other countries installing specialized factory floors. During those years, he and I never really connected like a father and son; we were more like friends working and doing drugs together.

By the time I was 23 years old, I was strung out on meth. I never thought I'd get addicted to drugs, but it snowballed out of control. I was hooked. That year, my dad sent my uncle and me to Oklahoma to do a big factory flooring job. Soon after arriving, I began having conflicts with my uncle. I was partying and doing drugs, then becoming belligerent with him when he tried to rein me in. During one particularly heated conflict, my uncle called the cops because I had threatened to beat him up. I wanted to get back to Florida, so I called my dad who bought me a plane ticket home. I started partying and missed the flight. I called my dad again, and he bought me another ticket. I missed that flight, too. The next time I called, he said he was done buying me tickets. So, I put a guilt trip on him saying, "You haven't known me my entire life and now you're telling me you've done enough for me?" So, he bought me another ticket. I didn't make that flight either.

Looking back, I see I was supposed to stay in Oklahoma because something important needed to happen there. I committed a robbery and ran over the victim while leaving the crime scene. While I was waiting to be transported to prison, I started a riot and set a mattress on fire and was sentenced to an additional 25 years with an 85% mandatory minimum sentence.

It was important to me to make a name for myself in this prison, so I went in as a tough guy, getting tattoos and starting fights to prove myself. My dad put money in my canteen account that I used to buy drugs to sell to the inmates. I was in tight with all the gang leaders. The only problem was all the fights I was involved in caused years to be added to my sentence. I was serving my sentences backward, adding years instead of subtracting them. I would be over 40 when I got out of prison. It sounded like an eternity.

For seven years straight, my dad wrote me letters. Letter after letter after letter. My dad had found Jesus and turned his life around and wanted the same for me. But I didn't grow up with religion. My mom and stepdad called stories about God and Jesus "Star Wars stories," and that's what I believed. I didn't want to read what he had to say, so I didn't open most of the letters. My cellmates told me they would love to get just one letter from their family, and here I was refusing to read the letters I got every single week.

My dad started coming to see me, traveling all the way from Florida to spend one hour talking to me through a thick pane of glass. He wanted to tell me about Jesus. I was seeing a different side of him I had never known, but I thought it was just more of his lies. I wasn't receiving his message, but I did convince him to smuggle drugs into the prison. I was putting him, his family, and his livelihood in jeopardy. Looking back, I realize it was selfish and wrong for me to do that.

One day, my dad heard from the Lord to "Go feed my sheep," so he told my stepmom to put $200 into my canteen account. Then God spoke to him again and said, "No! Go feed my sheep." It was the first time my dad had ever received a message from God, and this time he told my stepmom to buy him a ticket to Oklahoma. She got him a ticket, but before he was scheduled to leave, I was placed in segregation for having a guard bring in drugs. Inmates cannot have visitors if they're in segregation, so I sent word to him through my caseworker not to come. He came anyway.

Two Fathers Who Would Not Give Up

When my dad got to the prison, the guards told him he could not see me. Dad responded by asking for the warden's phone number. The guards told him the warden was on vacation. Dad again asked for the warden's phone number. He was not giving up. Eventually, the guards gave my dad the number, and he called the warden. After talking with my dad, the warden agreed to allow a one-hour visit. This was unheard of.

Here's how bitter and nasty my heart was at that time: When they came and told me I had a visitor, I said, "What? I can't have a visitor. I'm in segregation." When they told me it was my father, I got angry that he came because he wasn't going to be able to pass me drugs through the glass. What was he thinking coming here? I was annoyed and frustrated, not at all happy about this whole situation.

When I went into the visiting room, my dad was sitting and looking at me with tears in his eyes. I said roughly, "Why do you keep coming and visiting me?" He looked at me, and for the first time in my life, I thought he was speaking the truth when he said, "Because I love you, son. Because God told me to go feed my sheep, and all you ever needed to know was that I, your father, love you." Right then, at that very moment, God changed my heart. He turned my heart of stone into a heart that could accept unconditional love.

I began to weep. I looked at my dad and said, "Dad, I want what you've got. I want to know how you can love the unlovable and not give up on them." My dad led me through a prayer, and before the end of our visit, I turned my life over to Jesus.

Soon after, I was put into a Faith and Character program in another pod in the prison. Even though I had accepted Jesus, I was still getting high. Drugs had a strong hold on me, and this caused me to get in trouble. They had a policy that if you broke any of their rules, you got kicked out of the program, so I went to see the chaplain to quit before I got thrown out. He looked at me and said, "I don't know what kind of people you've known your whole life, but I'm not one of them. I'm not going to give up on you, and I'm not going to let you give up on yourself. I don't care how many write-ups you get; I'm not letting you out of my program. I see Jesus Christ in you."

I broke down and said, "Look, I'm high right now. I've been doing drugs and selling drugs in your pod. I've got an illegal cellphone in my cell, but I'm trying, and I want to quit so badly. I've tried everything."

The chaplain looked at me and said, "You haven't tried Jesus. He won't take something you won't freely give Him. You've got to give it to Him." I went back to my cell and wrote down a long fervent prayer to Jesus. I told Him, "I don't want to be a slave to addiction anymore. I want to be free from the bondage I'm living in, and if you are real, I want you to take this from me because I cannot do this on my own." Suddenly I felt completely different. From that day on, I've never done another drug and never smoked another cigarette. Not once. His love completely took the desire from me.

I was free from addiction, but the inmates who depended on my supply of drugs were not, and they soon turned against me. Six gang members came to kill me. They cornered me, and although I'm a big guy, I was one against many. They beat me to the ground and several inmates began jumping on me, targeting my head. I lay there thinking, "Is this what it's like to be a Christian?"

I ended up in the Intensive Care Unit for three days. They had to drain blood off my brain. I had a broken jaw, broken ribs, and detached retinas in both eyes. As I recovered, I told God I was not going to forsake Him, and when I was well enough to go back to prison, I felt God leading me to go back to that same facility. I could have requested to be sent to a different facility, but I went back to those same guys who had almost killed me and walked right up to them and said, "I forgive you." They were astonished.

It wasn't long before the men I had been leading in the wrong direction began following me in the right direction. God began to use me in a powerful way to lead people to Christ. I started studying the word of God trying to learn everything I could about Jesus. I became an inmate chaplain and used my love of God to create opportunities instead of opposition.

Today I'm out of prison and using my transformation to be an inspirational speaker at churches, on Facebook, and for youth groups. And I am always happy to testify to people I meet while working on their floors. I am called to share my story wherever I can.

 My message is no matter how much you feel like giving up on somebody, don't. Someone who will not change today, may change tomorrow. It can happen so quickly. For me, the moment of my transformation came about because of the combination of my father's love and God's love breaking open my heart. I walked into that prison visiting room where my father was patiently waiting for me that day as one kind of man and walked out a completely different man. My heart is full of peace and joy, thanks to the love of my two fathers.

Zack's dad, Tony, died of Covid two months after Zack was released from prison. Before he died, Tony watched a video of Zack on Facebook telling his story to a local church group. This is what he wrote in the Comment section, his final letter to his son:

I will never grow tired of listening to your story, son – to our story – to God's story.

No father on the planet could be prouder of their son than I am of you, my beautiful Zackery – you have inspired me in ways that have led me into the arms of Jesus over and over and over again. When I see you, I see a beautiful likeness of Christ poured out for all of us to partake of.

You have so much to offer the world around you, I cannot begin to fathom all that He has for us as a father and a son – I am a truly blessed man, and I thank God every day that He has brought my precious son home, whole and complete, as a new creation in Christ.

And for that, I shout Hallelujah and praise the Lord!

Reflection:

- Zack's dad never gave up on him and went to great lengths over and over to get through to Zack even though he had little encouragement. Who is someone in your life who would not give up on you?

- Consider this Bible passage from Luke 15:

  Rejoice with me because I found my lost sheep. In the same way, there is more joy in heaven over one lost sinner who repents and returns to God than over ninety-nine others who are righteous and haven't strayed away! –Luke 15:6

  How does this passage relate to Zack's story?

Susan
Angel of the Chemo Lab

I am something of a conundrum. On the one hand, I am more fit than 95% of women my age. On the other hand, my parents were told I may not live twice before I reached the age of twenty, and over the years, I have had more medical issues and surgeries than most people my age. None of my diagnoses have killed me, but some of them have certainly tried.

My cardiologist once told me that anybody who looks like they've never had a scratch on them but has a medical history like mine must *do* something with that. Up to that point, I thought I was doing a good job avoiding any impulse to drag my medical problems behind me like a coffin. But *do* something? What was I supposed to do with my medical experiences? I couldn't think of anything, so I didn't do anything.

Then fate struck again. I learned that how I respond to a situation, no matter how unpleasant, can impact people with similar problems. I became a person who could listen to the fear and anxiety of people with serious illnesses and calm their fears. When their fears become more than they can bear, I can offer them a shoulder to cry on. Here is how I got there.

In the summer of 2016, I was diagnosed with both breast and kidney cancer. Having two separate, unrelated cancers at the same time was overwhelming, so when a friend suggested I have a few sessions with a Christian life coach, I agreed.

Because Jim and I had just moved to a small coastal community before my diagnosis, we had not settled on a church home and didn't have a relationship with a local pastor. I made some inquiries and decided to talk with a delightful lady named Sharon. As a Christian Life Coach, she was able to talk with me from a Christian perspective about my worries and how to use my faith in this unsettling situation. That was what I needed, and we had a good first meeting.

Because our community had no medical facilities, I had to go to a small satellite chemo lab a few miles inland. The infusion room there was just big enough for eleven recliners placed side by side with a narrow tray between each. There was no room for friends or family to be in the room with the patients; there was barely enough room for the nurses and their carts. That day and every Wednesday morning for the next five months, I would be there with six men, chair against chair, with absolutely no privacy. All the men looked at their hands throughout the two or three hours we were there that first day. No one said a word, and the atmosphere reeked of misery. I shared all this with Sharon during my next visit.

She looked at me and said, "I know what you have to do. You have to become the angel of the chemo lab." I stared at her. She didn't understand. Nobody talked in that room. Nobody made eye contact. Sharon was undeterred. She repeated, "You have to become the angel of the chemo lab." I protested. I wouldn't know what to say. Or I would say the wrong thing. I was too reserved. I was too wounded. Her response was to tell me she knew that God wanted me to be the angel of the chemo lab, and I needed to put it in His hands to show me how to do it. I remained unconvinced.

The next Wednesday morning, I prepared for round two of chemo. I had discovered a metallic taste, like drinking water from a warm tin can, came into my mouth mere seconds after the infusion began. This time I prepared for that terrible taste by bringing a baggy full of a variety of hard mints, hoping to find at least one type that would counteract that awful sensation. I also packed a book, my journal, and a book of devotions to help pass the time. I was ready for the treatment but still didn't know what to do about Sharon's directive. As I walked in the door of the oncology office, I prayed, "God, if you want me to be the angel of the chemo lab, you need to open a door. If you open it, I'll walk through it."

I had just gotten settled into my recliner and was sorting through my tote bag when the nurse came over to the man seated on my right and said, "Mr. Lawrence, it's time to start your infusion." As she was preparing for the infusion, he muttered, "Oh Lord, I hate that taste that comes in my mouth. Please take that taste from me." My head jerked up. I grabbed my baggy and offered him his choice of mints. While he made his selections, I looked up and noticed that no one was looking at their hands; everyone was looking at the mints. Since I was not yet tethered to an infusion bag, I got up and offered mints to the rest of the men.

When I sat back down, Mr. Lawrence introduced himself and we became Ray and Susan. Ray asked me if he was correct that I was reading from a devotional the previous week and if I had brought it with me. I answered that I had. It was a book of devotions for people battling cancer. I pulled it out of my tote bag, and he asked if I would read today's lesson to myself and then state the message in one sentence. The message that day was, "*Whether* I lived or died was up to God, but *how* I lived was up to me."

As Ray and I began talking about the message, one of the men chimed in with a comment, then another man spoke up. Two weeks later, everyone was part of the discussion. By week four, the discussions continued long after we had dissected the devotion. We talked about everything: our fears, our tears, our worries, and our struggles.

Everything about the chemo lab had changed. Well, everything and nothing. We all had the same cancers, the same treatments, and the same prognoses, but now we were facing this ordeal together. I was struck with the realization we were an unlikely group. We were of different ages and races and had a wide range of occupations and education levels. Cancer had brought us together and was our common enemy. All our differences fell away as we shared our common experiences.

On my last day, one of the men asked if anyone else had uncontrollable gas three days after having chemo. We spent the next twenty minutes talking about passing gas and chuckling at some of the stories. We had come a long way from the days of everyone looking at their hands and saying nothing!

A couple of weeks after my chemo ended, I returned to the cancer center to have some blood work done. When I arrived at the check-in desk, the receptionist looked up and said, "Oh, it's you! Hold on a minute." Then she got up and went to the doorway of the infusion lab and called out, "Hey everybody! Mrs. Pyron is here!" I stood there, confused. This was not the usual check-in procedure. What was that about? She explained that "my guys" had been waiting for me, and the oncologist was making an exception by allowing me to go back to the infusion room for a short visit. When I walked into the room, every man looked up with a big smile on his face. I knew smiles were hard to come by in the chemo lab, so at that moment, it hit me. I really had become the angel of the chemo lab. I had done it, and it had all started with a mint and a prayer. God had, indeed, opened a door for me and in doing so, transformed my fellow patients into cherished friends.

Reflection:

- When has God opened a door for you when you needed it? Did you recognize it as a God moment at the time?

- Has God ever called you to do something you felt unqualified to do and found that God gave you the tools to answer that calling? Share with the group.

- Many people who do mission work say that they got more from it than they gave. What are the benefits to us when we help other people?

Finding Hope in the Middle
of a Personal Crisis

The light shines in the darkness, and the darkness can never extinguish it. -John 1:5

Some of the stories in this book hit the extreme edges of what you may have encountered in your life. We chose these stories because they demonstrate that whether you caused your problems, or they were thrust upon you, there is a way through it, no matter how extreme. Every person in this book overcame the issue that was pulling them into darkness, and they did it because of the faith in God they developed in their youth or in later years while in the throes of a life-altering experience.

There is something about having an experience that knocks your feet out from under you and brings you to your knees that makes a person humble. Humble enough to ask for help. Battered enough to know you cannot do this alone. In the Sermon on the Mount, Jesus said, "Blessed are the meek for they will inherit the earth." We are never so close to God than when we are at our lowest point. He is never so ready to pick us up than when we need him the most. It is in our darkest hours that we have our greatest chance to develop a relationship with God and start a brand-new journey. All we have to do is ask. And if we mess up and fail again, He will take us back as many times as we need. He is a God of infinite chances right up to the moment of our final breath. That's how much He loves us.

No matter what you've done or what you've suffered, there is hope. If you ask, God will be there with you every step of the way. Even if you think you don't deserve it, God thinks you are worthy. The light WILL shine in the darkness.

Acknowledgments

Bill and I are so grateful to all of you who were willing to share your story. It was our privilege to be allowed to sit with you as you recounted a difficult time in your life. Thank you for trusting us to represent you fairly and accurately. Whether your story made it into this book or not, you will always hold a special place in our hearts.

Jim Pyron, you were the first person to read my draft of every piece in this book. Just like everything in my life, I look to you first. Thank you for your excellent judgment and for having my back today, tomorrow, and forever.

Liz McBroom, I thank God for giving you to me as a daughter. I am constantly amazed at your wisdom and ability to cut through the noise and see what is important. Thank you for your insight and suggestions for this book. You make everything better just by being a part of it.

Chris Phelps, thank you for forty years of friendship and camaraderie. You are one of the kindest people I know, even though life hasn't always been kind to you. We've worked together, played together, and traveled together, so when I needed a proofreader and someone to give me honest feedback on the stories, I knew you were the perfect person. During a time of great grief from losing your beloved partner of almost 30 years, you put aside your troubles and came and helped me when I needed you. Thank you for sharing your time and talents with me both at work and in retirement.

Ann Adams, thank you for being my muse and North Star as well as trusted friend for almost forty years. Even though I moved 500 miles away, you have been available on the phone whenever I needed to find clarity or lost my way during the writing of this book. Your feedback and suggestions were invaluable to finding the common thread in these stories. You have been sorely tested in this life with growing up with an alcoholic father, having breast cancer, and now living with the physical disabilities of advanced Parkinson's. You are an inspiration and model in how to navigate a difficult situation with grace, never losing your gift of raining love down on your friends, family, and everyone you meet.

Natalie Glendenning, thank you for your editing and formatting help. Your comments about Jason's story two years ago helped me find clarity on what kind of stories people your age would want to read, and I couldn't have finished this book without your help. I am so proud of where you are in your life right now and know that there are many good things ahead of you.

Mace Crowe, you are so wise and good with words. You often made a comment in our small group that inspired and guided me with this book. If you find an occasional sentence in this book that reminds you of something you said, you're right. Thank you for giving me permission to use your insights.

Bill, thank you for being a first-rate idea man, editor and mentor. During the two and a half years we worked on this book, you have become a cherished friend and confidant as well as an honorary father. Your unfailing cheerfulness and unshakeable faith that rises above the unspeakable tragedy in your past and sustains you as you live with the difficult challenges of advanced Parkinson's disease will serve as a shining example to me for the rest of my life.

Susan Pyron grew up in Eden, North Carolina, a small textile town. She graduated from UNC-Chapel Hill in 1973 with a degree in English Education. During her years teaching in the public schools, she earned a master's degree in both Library Science and Reading at UNC-Greensboro.

After retirement, she and her husband Jim moved to Cortez, Florida where they both are involved in volunteer work with nonprofit organizations. In her position as a board member of a community foundation, she met Bill Laney. That meeting eventually led to the creation of this book.

Bill Laney grew up in Seattle, Washington and received a bachelor's degree in business administration and an ROTC Air Force Commission from the University of Michigan. He and his wife Suki moved from Seattle to Florida more than twenty years ago and were foster parents for many years. They have been married for over 50 years and raised five children, including two adopted Korean daughters.

Bill has been an active member of the Bayside Community Church for over twenty years. He is also a founding member of the Upper Room Community Foundation. His commitment to family, business innovation, and spiritual growth defines him as a remarkable individual with a lasting impact on those around him.

Made in the USA
Columbia, SC
20 December 2024

50209975R00051